SAVE THAT FOR A SUNNY DAY
WORKBOOK

BY X'ERNONA WOODS

XWOODS ENTERPRISE PUBLISHERS

Published by XWOODS ENTERPRISE
Chicago, Illinois 60649* xernona@gmail.com

International Standard Book Number:
978-0-9823886-1-7
Printed in the United States of America
This is a lead free publication.

FOREWORD

DOES MONEY GROW ON TREES?

There will always be a demand for money no matter what corner of the world you live in. It seems as if the cliche " Money Makes The World Go Around" proves to be true as evidence of the unfortunate downfall of the economy.

"Save That Penny For A Sunny Day" embraces the areas of economics, finance and budgeting and dispells the thought that the acronym 'ATM' is often defined by a large percentage of youth as 'Automatically Tell Mom.'

"Save That Penny For A Sunny Day" is not the cure but will offer a healing to those who understand what we are taught as youth often shadows our adulthood lives. Being strong stewards of our money is one way to start the healing process one household, one school, one after-school program at a time.

"Save That Penny For A Sunny Day" combined with academic components and national and state standards that focus on reading, math, and social studies to further enrich student learning opportunities while providing inter-related activities to support their cognitive and critical thinking skills.

Students will develop an understanding of how to utilize the teachings within "Save That Penny For A Sunny Day" for a lifetime to come.

After all, Money Really Doesn't Really Grow On Trees.

**Mr. Jesse White
Secretary of State**

IDENTIFY

Identify the president on each bill.

Benjamin Franklin = not a U.S. President

Dollar bill

Five-dollar bill

Twenty-dollar bill

Fifty-dollar bill

One hundred-dollar bill

4

REASONS
List ten reasons why you should save money.

1. _____

2. _____

3. _____

4. _____

5. _____

6. _____

7. _____

8. _____

9. _____

10. _____

MATCH
Match the money with its correct sum.

Four quarters
Ten dimes and one penny
Two quarters

CIRCLE
Circle the correct answer

1. Which sum is equal to a dollar?

a. Four quarters
b. Ten dimes
c. Two quarters

2. What is the sum of the four coins?

a. Sixty five cents
b. Fifty cents
c. Fourty-nine cents

3. What is the sum of four quarters, two dimes and six nickels?

a. One dollar
b. One dollar and fifty cents
c. Two dollars and fifty cents

4. What is the sum of six pennies and twenty dimes?

a. Sixteen cents
b. Two dollars and six cents
c. Twenty-six cents

5. What is the sum of four nickels and sixteen pennies?
a. Fourty-six cents
b. Twenty-six cents
c. Fourty cents

6. What is the sum of thirty nickels?
a. One dollar and fifty cents
b. Twenty-five cents
c. Three dollars

Name each coin

_____   _____   _____   _____

CHORES/PRICES

**Write a list of chores and the amounts
you will charge for your services.**

Examples
Take out trash.
Get the newspaper.
Set the dinner table.

_____

_____

_____

_____

_____

_____

_____

Divide the room between coupon cutters and non-coupon cutters.

Both groups should have the same amount: $50.00.

**Students will purchase pretend products with and without coupons
Products can be cut from old magazines and placed in
various areas of the room.**

**How much did the coupon cutters save versus
the non-coupon cutters?**

$1.50 off Sara Lettie Bread
Regular Price $3.00

Cheese $1.79
Regular Price $3.70

$1.00 off gallon of milk
Regular Price $3.99

T-Bone steak $4.89
Regular Price $7.99

2 for $1.00 Beef Frank Hotdogs
Regular Price $2.59

Pre-cooked rice $1.00
Regular Price $1.50

3 for a dollar potato chips
Regular price $1.70 per bag

Broccoli $2.50
Regular price $3.00

Chocolate chip cookies $1.29
Regular Price $3.00

Cream of chicken soup $1.85
Regular Price $ 2.80

Coco Crunchies cereal $3.50
Regular Price $5.59

Eggs $1.50
Regular Price $2.59/dozen

IMAGINATION
Imagination leads to creation

If you could create a new way to travel, what would it be?
If you could create a toy, what would it be?
Draw a picture of your creation.

Examples
Ten foot doll
Space ship

TALENTS AND INTEREST
List and describe your talents and interests.

_____

_____

_____

_____

_____

_____

_____

_____

_____

_____

_____

_____

SUPPORT

Support for the parents and teachers.

Encourage your students to start their own business with the use of the business plan provided within the workbook and compete with other classes. Judge competition based on business plan and the profits of business.

Develop career awareness. Field trips help children to learn about their environment and, more importantly, exposes youth to the possibilities of many careers. Teach children how different people in different places earn a living.

Arrange a field trip to the car dealership listed in the back of resource guide to see all the different jobs that are done in that one business building.

NEEDS & WANTS
Students should learn the power of making decisions.

Do you really need the latest video game?
Can you purchase the video game at a resale video store?
What are your short- and long-term goals?

_____

_____

_____

_____

_____

_____

PRETEND AND PLAY

Children will choose an occupation and dress like the worker they would like to become.

Examples: Nurse, videocast director, entrepreneur, actress, journalist, writer, fire person, police person, doctor, lawyer, engineer, builder, computer analyst, sports star, teacher, truck driver, bus driver, waiter or waitress, pharmacist, funeral director, politician, scientist, beautician or barber, funeral director, pastor, etc.

Students should write about their occupation by answering the following questions.

Why did you choose this occupation?
What is your desired salary?
What is needed to become the occupation you choose?
Example: Degree

_____

_____

_____

_____

_____

_____

_____

_____

POSITIVE AFFIRMATION
Create a contract.

I am rich.
I am happy.
I am successful.
I am worthy.
I am priceless.

_____

_____

_____

_____

_____

_____

_____

_____

_____

_____

WHERE?

Where does my money go?
Write the amount of money you receive for allowance?
Write within the circle graph how much is money is needed to budget your allowance.

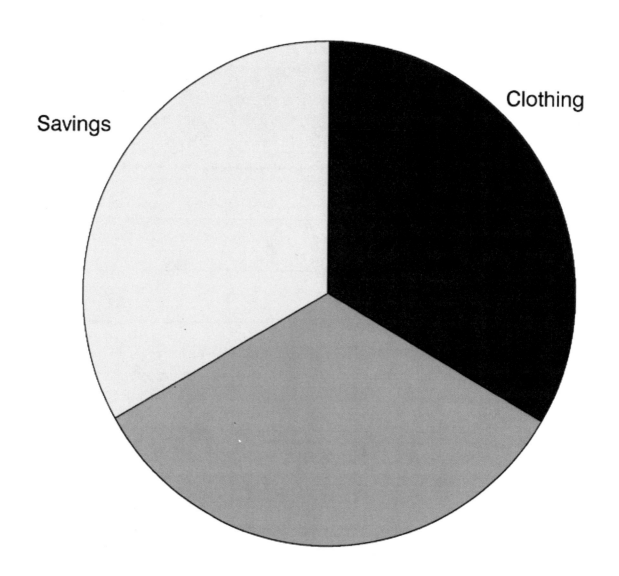

DEFINITION
Match the words with the definitions.

Trademark

A peculiar distinguishing mark or device affixed by a manufacturer or a merchant to his goods, the exclusive right of use of which is registered with the federal government and recognized by law.

Advertise

A grant made by the federal government that confers upon the creator of an invention the sole right to make, use, or sell that invention for a set period of time.

Earnings

The purpose toward which an endeavor is directed: an objective.

Money

To give public notice of to announce publicly, especially by printed notice; as in "to advertise goods for sale."

Salary or wages. Business profits. Gains from investments.

Goals

A medium that can be exchanged for goods and services and is used as a
measure of their values on the market; included among its forms are commodities such as gold, an officially issued coin or note, or a deposit in a checking account or other readily liqueafiable account.

Patent

Profits

A document prepared by a company's management, detailing the past, present,
and future of the company, usually designed to attract capital investment.

Networking

Exhange of information or services among individuals, groups or institutions.

What is left from earnings after all expenses have been provided.

Business plan

MAP
Savings Map was designed to support their vision of their heart desires.

Materials needed: Old magazines, scissors, green construction paper.

Directions: Cut out various pictures that reflect what you desire from life.
Example: Car, house, family and occupation.

STORY

Use the following words to write a short story about your success.

1. Money   _____
2. Investment
3. Savings   _____
4. College
5. Entrepreneurship   _____
6. Mutual Funds
7. Idea   _____
8. Net Worth
9. Value   _____
10. Deserve

_____

_____

_____

_____

_____

_____

_____

_____

_____

_____

HOW MUCH CAN YOU AFFORD?

How much house can you afford?

Billy earns $75,000 a year as a police officer; he wants to purchase a three-bedroom condo for $275,000. Can he afford this condo? Bill's mortgage payment is $2,500.00.

To figure how much Bill earns monthly, divide his salary by 12.

Bill monthly expenses are:

$600.00 rent $30.00 Personal tolietries
$300.00 auto loan $70.00 Recreation
$100.00 car insurance $45.00 Charity
$150.00 gas and light $200.00 Savings
$75.00 groceries
$50.00 credit card
$100.00 gas
Add Bills total amount

Can he afford this house?

Sally earns $45,000 a year as a school counselor. She wants to purchase a two bedroom house for $99,000. Can Sally afford the house? Sally's mortgage payment would be $800.00 a month.

To figure how much Sally earns monthly divide her salary by 12.

Sally's monthly expenses are:

$500.00 rent $45.00 Charity
$200.00 auto loan
$50.00 car insurance
$80.00 groceries
$75.00 gas and light
Add Sally's total amount

Can she afford this house?

SCORING HIGH WITH YOUR CREDIT

Credit is trust with money or finances. Often, having a bad credit score is a reflection of how responsible you are with budgeting. Did you know that having a bad credit can stop you from buying a home or car? Bad credit can also increase the amount you might have to pay for your big-ticket items. Instead of purchasing the car for its true worth you will have to spend more money for interest than necessary if your credit were better. A credit card gives a person permission to purchase items without cash. Every month it is best to pay off the full amounts of your credit card bills to avoid paying unnecessary interest (the extra interest paid for longer borrowing of money). Also, pay on time to avoid late payment fees. A creditor is a person or company to whom you owe money.

How can credit affect your spending power?
What does it mean to have credit?
What is a credit card?
What is the role of the creditor?

AFFORD THE LIFESTYLE YOU WANT

Richard Thomson purchased a pre-owned, red convertible for $2,500.00. Richard's monthly expenses are rent $596.00, electricity $35.00, gas $109.00, car insurance $256.00. wardrobe $200.00, gas for car $120.00. Richard's net pay is $1,000.00 biweekly. Can Richard afford his lifestyle?

Lisa Lowry wants to travel to Brazil. The trip would cost $2,400.00. Lisa monthly expenses are $780 for mortgage, home insurance $145.00, car note $456.00, car insurance $124.00, gas for truck $150.00, electricity $68.00, gas for car $98.16, wardrobe $500.00, and groceries $125.67. Lisa's weekly pay is $1,267. Can Lisa afford the trip to Brazil?

Winston Montgomery wants to purchase a computer for $1,239.89. Winston's monthly expenses are $1,150 for mortgage, car note $408.00, car insurance $136, gas for car $120.00, credit card $30.00, day care expense $100.00, groceries $125.00, wardrobe for both his son and self $450, electricity $98.00, gas bill $78. Winston's pay monthly is $3,500.00. Can Winston afford a computer?

Create your own salary and write your expenses.
Can you afford the lifestyle you want?

_____

_____

_____

_____

_____

WHAT'S YOUR PASSION?

Do what you love and the money will follow. Marsha Sinetar, in the late 1980's, found that 95% of American workers disliked the work they did.

JOB SHADOWING

Parents and teachers can help youth gain experience by allowing students to visit their parents' jobs.

HOW SHE DID IT

The Body Shop owner, Anita Roddick, is a multi-millionaire who started The Body Shop in Brighton, England, with a loan of $6,500. The Body Shop produces cosmetics that are sold internationally in 1,500 stores in 46 countries.

Anita Roddick was born in the small English town of Littlehampton where she worked in the family café. She later graduated from the Maude Allen Secondary Modern School for Girls and almost pursued a career as an actress. Instead, Anita Roddick ventured to college where she major in English, history and art.

HOW HE DID IT

Twenty-one-year-old, self-made millionaire Farrah Gray tells how, through desperation after watching his mother experience a second heart attack due to stress, he, at the age of six, painted rocks and sold them as paperweights.

Later Gray's intellect led him to create an investment club with neighborhood kids and he raised $15,000 via investing in small local retailers. Currently, he is a motivational speaker, a member of the board of the National Association of Real Estate Brokers, and the best-selling author of *Reallionaire*. He was recently invited to a roundtable discussion with President Bush. Gray made his television debut when he was interviewed on Backstage Live. At the age of nine, he became a co-host; at the age of 14 he retired his mother and grandmother.

HOW SHE DID IT

Ms. J K Rowling was born on July 31st, 1965 in Chipping Sodbury, Gloucestershire, England. Her given name at birth was Joanee Kathleen It is interesting to note that Ms. Rowling claims that she has actually bee writing since was 5- or 6- years old. Her first story, called Rabbit, was filled with interesting characters, such as a large bee called Miss Bee.

Ms. Rowling met and married a journalist in Portugal, and her daughter Jessica was born in 1993. Shortly after the birth of her daughter, the marriage ended in divorce and Ms. Rowling along with her infant daughter, moved to Edinburgh, Scotland.

J K was determined to finish her Harry Potter wizard novel, and to get it published. Ms. Rowling requested a grant from the Scotish Arts Council, which she eventually received, in order to complete her book. When she completed and after several rejections, Ms. Rowling sold the novel, Harry Potter and The Philospher's Stone, to Bloomsbury in the UK for $4,000.

To support her daughter and herself, Ms. Rowling began working as a French teacher. After several months Arthur Levine Books/ Scholastic Press bought the American rights to the first " Harry Potter," and Ms. Rowling received enough to give up teaching and write full time.

By the summer of 2000, Ms. Rowling had reportedly earned over $400 million for her first three Harry Potter books, which have been printed in 35 languages and sold over 30 million copies. Her fourth book in the popular series, entitled Harry Potter and the Goblet of Fire, pre-sold over one million advanced copies, with a first printing of 5.3 million. Because of her domination and incredible success on the New York Times bestseller list, the decision was made to introduce a bestseller's list for children's books, which would eliminate the dominating factor of these bestsellers on the current The New York Times bestseller list.

HOW SHE DID IT

Vanessa and Angela Simmons

Following their family's successful example, the unstoppable Vanessa and Angela Simmons of MTV's "Run House" are quickly building the next household name with their popular Pastry Shoes brand. Like their Uncle Russell Simmons with his Phat Fashion brands and their father Joseph "Rev Run" Simmons with his Run Athletics brand, Vanessa and Angela are branching out to introduce clothes and handbag collections.

Make a list of what you love and how you can make money.

For example: Writing / Author
                     Drawing/ Cartoonist

_____

_____

_____

_____

_____

_____

_____

_____

_____

_____

_____

_____

SAVE THAT PENNY FOR A SUNNY DAY

BUSINESS PLAN

Business Plan

Karim wrote a business plan to help explain his business.
Follow the business plan to create your business.
Ask your parent or teacher for help.

In this module, you will develop a business plan for an entrepreneurial idea that you have. Your business plan should include the basics.

After studying the module you should be able to:

1. Provide three reasons why business plans are necessary for a new business or for a major modification of an existing business.

2. Identify the various sections of a business plan, explaining why they are necessary.

3. Develop business plans for businesses you would like to create.

A business plan focuses on particulars about establishing a new business or revising a current business. A business plan is useful for a variety of reasons which include:

The plan is necessary for gaining funding from most financial sources, even family and friends. The business plan helps to convince possible lenders to give you a loan. It can also be used to attract individuals to become partners in your firm.

The plan helps you think through various aspects of the business. By preparing the business plan, you can better tell if your idea is a good one. Some people get halfway through the business plan and realize their plan is not compatible to what they desire. It is better to start a business that is your passion – a business that makes you happy.

The plan can also serve as a guide for the operation of the business. The goals that you establish should be used as checkpoints for the firm. This does not mean that goals cannot change as time goes on. But it is important to have some guidelines by which you check the wealth of your firm as you go along.

Developing a business plan can be a fun activity because you are developing a plan in which you are thinking through how you will achieve your dreams. You should think about different sources for coming up with the content of the plan. Technical assistance can and should be used. Go to local library sources, teachers, and professional associations. Financial institutions will also be willing to help you in the development of the plan.

The idea that there is one perfect business plan that fits all businesses is not correct. A business plan cannot be mass produced; it must be custom designed by you! Your business plan will be different from another person's because you are a different person; your competition will be different, target market will be different, and your product and services will be different. Your business plan is like your life's story, different and unique from everyone else's.

There are a number of items that you will want to include in this section. Forms are available at the end of the module which include each of these important elements.

1. What is the name of the business? Make sure that the name is attractive to customers and is descriptive of the type of business that you are operating.

2. What is the purpose of the business? In this section, indicate what you plan to produce and/or sell?

3. Why did you choose this idea? One major factor to include in this section is whether there is any proof that the product or service that you are producing will sell. Put in this section any information which will prove that there is a demand for this type of item which is not being met. There might be some nationwide studies or articles which indicate that your idea is a very popular one throughout the nation or your region. Be sure to include references to such articles or studies.

4. Are there any unique qualities in the item that you are planning to produce and/or sell? Put in this section any qualities that your items will have that others will not have, especially those which are in direct competition with you?

5. Who will be your primary customers? Indicate such data as age, sex, income level, and perhaps educational level of your potential customers. If there is population data on the target market in library sources, be sure to include that data is in this section with citations

6. Where will your business be located? Indicate where you will run the project and why you have chosen that location. Is it because of customer traffic patterns, low cost, convenience for you, etc?

Qualifications of those who will be running the business:

1. They must have the skills needed for the business. In this section, indicate all the skills that you believe are necessary to make your business work. Include even those skills which you may not have at the present time.

2. Indicate the skills that you have and prove if possible why you believe you have those skills. For example, if you believe that you have sales skills, you may have sold the most raffle tickets for a class project.

3. Name the skills which others will be called upon to provide. If you do not have some of the skills mentioned in the first section, that's okay, but be sure to indicate where and how you will secure people who have these other skills. If you plan to bring a partner aboard, put in the skills that he/she will bring to the business. If you plan to hire someone to assume some of the activities that you are not very good at, describe the type of employee for which you will be looking. Also, indicate any volunteer labor available; some moms and dads may be helpful. Also, you should mention any other various sources of assistance on which you will rely to get business started.

THE NATURE OF THE COMPETITION

1. Who are the major competitors? List in this section the primary competitors in your general area and indicate why you believe that they are your major competitors.

2. Explain how you plan to beat the competition. In this section, there may be several options, such as better prices, better quality, and different marketing practices. Select those which best fit your business and explain how and why you will be using them.

MARKETING YOUR PRODUCT

In this section there is a series of decisions which should help you with your marketing plan.

They include:

1. Who is your target audience? There are several characteristics listed in this checklist which should help you identify your target audience. The descriptions should correspond with the section in the first part of the business plan which focuses on the target audiences/markets.

2. What information will help people make a decision to buy your items instead of the competitor's? For this checklist, you are asked to indicate factors which most influence your target audience. Then rank those factors in order of their importance.

3. Which sales tools and promotions are the best to use for your target audience? In this section, various tools should be listed. Check those which you believe should be used and explain why they should be used; also indicate any estimated costs to use these sales tools. Do the same for any sales promotion techniques you plan to use.

In the next section, you are asked to develop some actual sales tools for your product or service. Select those tools which you indicated should be used to sell your product or service. Keep in mind that you want to focus on concerns most important to the identified target audience, as indicated in Item #2 under Marketing Your Product.

COST OF GETTING STARTED

On a separate sheet of paper indicate what you will need to get started and how you can secure the items that you will need. The ending activity in this section focuses on how much money will be needed and where you plan to get that money.

PROJECTED REVENUE, COST AND PROFIT DATA

Before someone agrees to invest in a firm, he or she will want to know what the projected profitability of the business is. Provide that data for at least the first six months.

NATURE OF BUSINESS

Name of Business:

Business Plan Prepared By:

Date:

My business idea is:

(Describe the purpose of your business in one or two sentences.)
I chose this business idea because:

Unique qualities of what I am producing and or selling:

Who is my primary target audience?

Where is the business to be located?

SKILLS

The skills needed to make this idea work are:

Which of these skills and experiences do I have? My skills and experiences:

Who will offer any additional skills which I do not have?

Who will be the first person I go to for help in that area where Ineed more skills, experience, or advice?

(You may need to come back to this question several times as your business idea grows and you learn more about business and the kinds of people who are there to help you.)

Type of help needed: Advisor

LOOKING AT MY COMPETITION

My major competitors are:
(who, in your general area, does what you will be doing):

I plan to beat the competition by:

Better prices? Explain.

Better quality? Explain.

Providing door-to-door services?

MARKETING

In planning your sales promotion or program, you must make several major decisions.

You have to make all decisions before you begin selling your product?
Who is your target audience?

Who and where are your potential customers?

What ages are they?

What races are they?

How much money do they have?

Are they wealthy or poor?

Where do they live?

What are their interests?

What will attract them to your product?
Price? Quality? Service? Selection? You?

Made in the USA
Columbia, SC
19 December 2022

73663842R00020